DRAGONFLIES

Published by Smart Apple Media

123 South Broad Street

Mankato, Minnesota 56001

Copyright © 1999 Smart Apple Media.

Photos: Blair Nikula. Rob Day (page 10).

Entomological Society of America/Ries Memorial Slide

Collection (page 17).

Design &Production: EvansDay Design

Project management: Odyssey Books

Library of Congress Cataloging-in-Publication Data

Halfmann, Janet, 1944–

Dragonflies / Janet Halfmann. –1st ed.

p. cm. – (Bugs)

Includes bibliographical references and index.

Summary: Describes the habitat, life cycle, behavior,

predators, and unique characteristics of dragonflies.

ISBN 1-887068-32-5 (alk. paper)

1. Dragonflies–Juvenile literature.   [1. Dragonflies.]

I. Title. II. Series: Bugs (Mankato, Minn.)

QL520.H386 1998

595.7'33–dc21   98-15372

5 4 3 2

DRAGONFLIES

Janet Halfmann

PHOTOGRAPHS BY BLAIR NIKULA

Soar. DIVE. **ZOOM.** *LOOP THE LOOP.*

STOP ON A DIME! DRAGONFLIES ARE THE

STUNT FLIERS OF SUMMER. THEY *dart*

EVERY WHICH WAY, HUNTING MOSQUI-

TOES AND OTHER INSECTS ON THE WING.

THESE DRAGONS OF THE AIR ARE AS

glitzy AS THEY ARE DARING. LONG,

SLENDER BODIES *sparkle* WITH BRIGHT

COLORS—BLUE, GREEN, RED, BRONZE.

SHEER WINGS *shimmer* IN THE SUN-

LIGHT. THE DRAGONFLY'S COLORFUL AIR

SHOW HAS BEEN GOING ON FOR MILLIONS

OF YEARS. WHAT IS THE STORY OF THESE

BEAUTIFUL INSECT HAWKS OF SUMMER?

The Dragonfly's Family

Dragonflies belong to the ORDER, or group, of insects called *Odonata,* meaning "tooth." The name refers to the sharp teeth on their jaws. They earned their common name because they look like small winged dragons, with monstrous eyes, large saw-like jaws, and long tails or abdomens.

Besides dragonflies, the order *Odonata* includes damselflies. Dragonflies belong to the suborder *Anisoptera* and damselflies to the suborder *Zygoptera.* Dragonflies and

damselflies are closely related and similar in many ways. In fact, the word "dragonfly" is often used by people to mean both dragonflies and damselflies.

There are seven families of dragonflies in North America. The Skimmer family is the largest and most common; the Petaltail family is the smallest. Others are the Darners, Clubtails, Spiketails, Cruisers, and Emeralds.

There are five families of damselflies. The three most common are Pond Damsels, Spreadwings, and Broad-winged Damsels.

This Halloween Pennant belongs to the Skimmer family of dragonflies.

Older Than Dinosaurs

Giant dragonflies as big as crows, with wingspans of 28 inches (71 cm), flew through the sky 250 million years ago. That was long before the dinosaurs roamed the earth! Prehistoric dragonflies named *Meganeura* were the largest insects ever.

By the time of the dinosaurs, dragonflies were much like those we see today. They were among the first insects to fly, and even today they are one of the largest insects.

Dragonfly or Damselfly?

How can you tell a dragonfly from a damselfly? The easiest way is to look at their wings when they perch. Most dragonflies rest with their wings straight out, airplane style, and the back wings are wider than the front ones. All damselflies, except Spreadwings, perch with their wings held together above their bodies, and all four wings are the same size.

Also, the dragonfly has much larger eyes. They are so enormous that they sometimes touch across the middle of the head. The smaller eyes of the damselfly are far apart on either side of the head.

Dragonflies are generally larger and stouter, while damselflies are delicate and have very slender abdomens. Dragonflies are stronger fliers, while damselflies have a slower, fluttering flight.

Dragonflies hold their wings straight out when resting, and their large eyes cover much of the head. Most damselflies hold their wings together above the body, and their eyes are on the sides of the head.

Habitat

There are more than 5,500 SPECIES, or kinds, of dragonflies and damselflies. They live in all parts of the world where there is water, warm weather, and plenty of food. More than half of the species live in tropical climates like those of Latin America, Africa, Southeast Asia, and northern Australia. Japan also has many species.

North America has about 650 species. The most familiar is the Common Green Darner (*Anax junius*), one of the largest and swiftest dragonflies. It has clear wings

The spotted wings of the Twelve-spotted Skimmer flash in the sun as this familiar dragonfly flies over ponds in North America.

and a bright green head and thorax. Also common is the Twelve-spotted Skimmer (*Libellula pulchella*), easily recognized by the three large brown spots on each wing.

A well-known damselfly is the American Rubyspot (*Hetaerina americana*). The male's wings have bright red spots. Another common damselfly is the Ebony Jewelwing (*Calopteryx maculata*), named for the male's jet-black wings.

Dragonflies Like Water   Dragonflies are most often spotted flying about on a warm, sunny day near a lake or pond with plants growing along its banks. They can also be found near streams, bogs, marshes, waterfalls, and even puddles in leaves high up in tropical trees.

For example, the Common Green Darner and the Twelve-spotted Skimmer prefer ponds and other quiet waters. But the American Rubyspot and the Ebony Jewelwing favor fast waters ranging from brooks to rivers with rapids.

And which dragonfly grows up near waterfalls? That would be an African Hawker dragonfly named *Zygonyx*.

Dragonflies Are Sun-Lovers

Most dragonflies are sun-lovers. They need to be warm to fly. Early in the morning you might see them basking in the sun or quivering their wings to make their bodies warmer. On cloudy days, they cling to reed stems or the underside of leaves, not moving at all.

Body and Senses

Like many insects, the dragonfly has a tough outer covering (EXOSKELETON), which gives support and protection. Also, like all insects, the dragonfly has six legs and breathes air through tiny openings in the exoskeleton. Its body has three parts: head, thorax, and abdomen.

Like this Common Whitetail, the bodies of all dragonflies have three parts: head, thorax or chest, and abdomen.

Huge, Keen Eyes The dragonfly's large head is mostly eyes. Two huge, bulging eyes of bright red, green, or blue cover more than half of its head. They are the best eyes of any insect—perfect for hunting on the wing. Each eye has 28,000 lenses, compared to 4,000 in a housefly. The dragonfly can swivel its head all around and can spot a meal at 40 feet (12.2 m) in any direction!

The dragonfly has two ANTENNAE, or feelers, which are very tiny. The large jaws

The Common Green Darner's bulging eyes are so large that they meet on top of its head!

of the dragonfly contain saw-like teeth for chewing up insects. Its lower lip features a hook to grasp its prey.

The large THORAX, or chest, is filled mostly with wing muscles used to power the dragonfly's four powerful wings. It also contains the leg muscles, which control long, spine-covered legs with tiny hooked claws at the end. As the dragonfly flies, it holds its legs bunched up together near its mouth, forming a basket to scoop up insects—sometimes dozens at a time!

The dragonfly also uses its legs for perching, but they are not strong enough for walking.

Long, Colorful Abdomen   The dragonfly's ABDOMEN is long, narrow, and often brightly colored. It might be red, turquoise, green, purple, yellow, blue, or copper—sometimes with striking patterns. Males are generally more colorful than females.

The abdomen also holds the heart, reproductive organs, and digestive and breathing systems. The male has two claspers at the end of the abdomen that he uses to grasp the female when mating.

The dragonfly is an almost perfect flying machine. Scientists have studied it to learn the secrets of its amazing flight.

The abdomens of many Odonata are brightly colored, like that of the Delta Spotted Spiketail dragonfly pictured at left.

Dragons of the Air

If there were an Olympics for insects, the dragonfly would capture the gold medal. It is one of the fastest-flying insects, zooming through the air at 30 miles (48.2 km) per hour or more.

It can also dip and dive like a stunt pilot. No insect prey is safe. The dragonfly can turn somersaults, hover in midair like a helicopter, fly backward, turn sharply, even fly upside down if need be—anything to snare an insect meal!

Dragonfly wings are perfectly suited for flight. Unlike the wings of other insects, each pair works by itself. The two pairs of wings are long and narrow, and receive strength from a framework of veins. They

Most dragonfly wings average 3–4 inches (7.6–10 cm) from tip to tip. Some are even larger. The wings of the Borneo dragonfly (*Tetracanthagyma plagiata*) span 7 inches (17.8 cm)!

are usually transparent, but some feature colorful spots, bars, or tints.

As the wings beat, they twist and bend, giving extra lift. Scientists have studied dragonfly wings to learn why the dragonfly can fly so fast and perform such amazing acrobatics.

Hunting   Some dragonflies, such as the Darners, hunt by patrolling up and down an area, scooping up insects as they go. Others, such as the Skimmers and Clubtails, hunt from a sunlit lookout perch, darting out when they see an insect.

Dragonflies often wander far from their home pond or stream to hunt for food, but they return to mate and lay their eggs. Often the male will stake out a territory by cruising back and forth, chasing away other males.

Mating on the Wing When a female enters the male's territory, he pursues her. He can tell if she's the same species by her size, color, the pattern on her wings, and the way she flies.

When he catches her, he grasps the back of her head with his claspers. The male and female then fly attached together, with the male leading. The female bends her abdomen down and forward to connect with the male's abdomen. Their abdomens form a circle shape called a mating wheel. Sometimes, the shape even looks like a heart!

Most dragonflies, such as the Common Green Darner, mate on the wing. Other species, especially damselflies, perch on a nearby plant. Right after mating, the female lays her eggs.

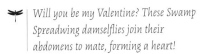 *Will you be my Valentine? These Swamp Spreadwing damselflies join their abdomens to mate, forming a heart!*

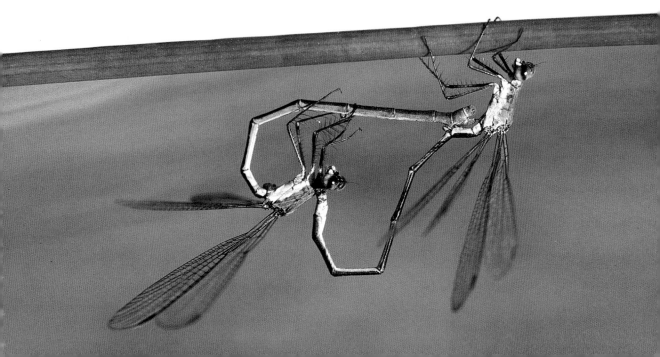

Life of the Dragonfly

The dragonfly's life has three stages: egg, nymph, and adult. This process of growth is called incomplete METAMORPHOSIS. Most insects, such as beetles and moths, go through a four-part change, which includes a pupal stage. This is called complete metamorphosis.

The Darner dragonfly pushes her eggs into a plant stem with her abdomen. They are long and sausage-shaped. Other dragonflies lay their eggs in the water. They are usually round.

Eggs Laid in Water   As the eggs come out of the tip of the female's abdomen, they are fertilized by the sperm she received from the male. Most female dragonflies lay their eggs in or near the water, but they do it in different ways.

Darner dragonflies and damselflies

push their eggs into the stems of water plants. Spiketail dragonflies force their eggs into the sand or gravel at the edges of shallow streams. Some Skimmers drop their eggs while flying above the water. Others skim the surface, dipping the tip of the abdomen in the water to wash off the eggs.

Most male dragonflies stay with the females as they lay their eggs, chasing away other males and protecting their mates from enemies. The Common Green Darner and many damselflies stay attached to the female as she lays her eggs. Others release the female but stay nearby. For example, the Common Whitetail dragonfly (*Libellula lydia*) hovers above the female as she lays her eggs.

The number of eggs varies from a few hundred for species that put them in plants

The Killer Lip

When looking for a meal, a nymph hides in the mud or among water weeds. When it spots prey, it creeps close. Then it shoots out its lip at lightning speed. The lip can be half as long as its body! Hooks on the end of the lip grab the prey and pull it to the nymph's mouth. The lip then folds up. It's called a mask because it covers most of the nymph's face. No other insect has this killer lip.

to a few thousand for species that drop them in the water. Most eggs hatch within 7 to 30 days, depending on the warmth of the water. Soon after mating and egg-laying are done, most adult dragonflies die. They have only been adults a few weeks.

Nymphs Are Pond Monsters! A tiny, drab, rather ugly creature called a NYMPH hatches from the egg. It has a big head and mouth, large eyes, two antennae, six long legs, and no wings.

It breathes through a gill chamber inside the abdomen. Water is sucked into the end of the abdomen and washes over the gills to provide oxygen.

The gill chamber also gives the nymph a speedy way to escape from enemies or chase down prey. If water is forced rapidly out of the chamber, the nymph propels forward like a jet. A Common Green Darner nymph can speed up to 20 inches (50.8 cm) per second!

Damselfly nymphs differ from their dragonfly cousins. They are more slender and delicate, and have three tail-like gills. They swim by moving the abdomen from side to side like a fish.

The nymphs are so ferocious and hungry that they are sometimes called "pond monsters." They aren't fussy eaters. They gobble up anything smaller than they are, and sometimes even attack larger creatures. They eat mostly water insects and larvae, but as they get larger, they snare tadpoles, small fish, and even other nymphs.

Soon, the hungry nymph's skin gets too tight. No problem! The skin splits, and the nymph wriggles out of it. A new larger skin is underneath. This process is called MOLTING. All insects molt, usually about five times. But dragonfly and damselfly nymphs molt 10 to 15 times!

After the third or fourth molt, tiny wing pads appear. The nymph gradually begins to look more and more like an adult.

For most nymphs, this growing process

 The nymph is a hungry, ferocious eater. It even gobbles up creatures larger than itself.

takes one to two years. The Common Green Darner takes one year, and many European species take two years.

When the nymph is about 2 inches (5 cm) long, it stops eating. This is a signal that a big change is about to take place.

Time to Fly　On a summer night, the nymph leaves the water and crawls up a plant, log, or rock. Its skin splits and the new adult pulls its body out of the skin. It is a mighty struggle. The dragonfly is soft and its wings are crumpled. Then the wings expand and the abdomen stretches. The new dragonfly waits for its wings and body to dry.

When the sun comes up, the dragonfly is ready to fly. It flies away from the water to the fields, trees, or woods. It needs time to MATURE, or finish growing up. During this time, its body and wings harden, its colors get darker and brighter, and its reproductive organs develop. It will take up to a month for the dragonfly to fully mature.

This Mottled Darner is changing from a nymph into an adult. Soon it will stretch its wings and fly.

Setting Up a Mating Territory

Male dragonflies mature before the females. This gives them time to return to the water first and set up a mating territory. Soon the females return to the water, too. When dragonflies and damselflies return to the water, they are ready to mate. Soon there will be new eggs waiting to hatch, and the life process will start all over again.

Dragonfly Enemies

Danger for dragonflies starts even before the eggs hatch. One dragonfly enemy is a tiny wasp called a fairy-fly. She finds the dragonfly eggs underwater, and puts one of her own eggs in each one. Soon the fairy-fly eggs hatch, and the larvae eat the insides of the dragonfly eggs.

For dragonfly nymphs that do hatch, the dangers continue. The nymphs are on the menus of waterbirds, frogs, water snakes, and especially fish. Many water insects also eat nymphs. And dragonfly nymphs sometimes eat one another!

For the nymph that grows up and

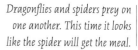

Dragonflies and spiders prey on one another. This time it looks like the spider will get the meal.

leaves the water, the danger only increases. During the time the nymph is changing into an adult, it is helpless—it cannot move or protect itself. Darkness makes it safer for some, but still many nymphs get eaten at night by spiders, fish, birds, or even crocodiles.

From Hunter to Hunted   The adult dragonfly can escape from most enemies by its speed and acrobatics. But sometimes the hunter becomes the hunted. Many birds, including swallows and hawks, are on the lookout for dragonflies. Frogs and toads find dragonflies tasty, too. Female dragonflies often get snatched by fish while laying their eggs in the water.

A Dragonfly Needs a Home

Dragonflies have become scarce or have disappeared in certain areas. That's because the water has become polluted or wetlands have been drained or filled in for development.

People can help by working to keep water clean, and by creating new ponds to replace water habitats that have been destroyed. Dragonflies will usually adopt a new water habitat. They have even been known to take over outdoor pools!

Even though dragonflies have lots of enemies, they have managed to survive for millions of years. They are not likely to run out of food because they eat so many kinds of insects. Dragonflies also are not fussy and will adapt to many clean water habitats.

In fact, the number of dragonflies near a body of water can tell scientists about the quality of the environment. That's because both adult and baby dragonflies need a lot of food to survive. So, the presence of a large number of dragonflies means many other animals are doing well in that environment, too.

Dragonflies and Us

In the past dragonflies have been called "devil's darning needles" or "snake doctors." That's because these names and others come from old stories about dragonflies sewing up the mouths of naughty children, or bringing snakes back from the dead.

Of course, none of these stories are true.

Yes, the slender body of a dragonfly does resemble a needle or a stinger, but dragonflies are completely harmless. They don't sting or bite, except to eat insects that bite and sting us.

The abdomen of this Scarlet Bluet damselfly looks like a stinger, but it isn't. Neither dragonflies nor damselflies bite humans.

Mosquito Hawk One dragonfly nickname that does fit is "mosquito hawk." Both dragonfly adults and babies eat lots of mosquitoes. Sometimes an adult dragonfly's mouth gets so full of mosquitoes that it can't even close its jaws! That's good news for us.

Dragonflies eat many other bothersome insects, too, like midges, gnats, and flies. Both the adults and babies are meat-eaters. They never eat plants. Once in a while, though, dragonflies are a nuisance. Dragonfly nymphs sometimes eat lots of baby fish, endangering fish populations. In the southeastern United States, the large Common Green Darner and the Regal Darner (*Coryphaeshna ingens*) are serious PREDATORS of honeybees.

Yet overall, dragonflies are our friends. So the next time you're near a pond or stream on a warm summer day, sit quietly for a while and watch the dragons of the air. You'll be treated to a beautiful and daring air show that has been millions of years in the making.

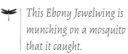

This Ebony Jewelwing is munching on a mosquito that it caught.

BOOKS

Discovering Damselflies and Dragonflies, Linda Losito, The Bookwright Press, 1988

Dragonflies, Cynthia Overbeck, Lerner Publications Company, 1982

Dragonflies, Heather Amery, Gareth Stevens Publishing, 1996

Dragonflies, Hidetomo Oda and Jun Nanao, Raintree Publishers, 1986

Dragonflies, Hilda Simon, The Viking Press, 1972

Dragonflies, Molly McLaughlin, Walker and Company, 1989

Dragonflies, Oxford Scientific Films, G.P. Putnam's Sons, 1980

Dragonflies and Damselflies, Mary Geisler Phillips (degree in biology), Thomas Y. Crowell Company, 1960

Dragonfly, Emery Bernhard, Holiday House, 1993

Dragonfly, Barrie Watts, Silver Burdett Press, 1988

The Dragonfly over the Water, Christopher O'Toole, Gareth Stevens Publishing, 1988

Green Darner, the Story of a Dragonfly, Robert M. McClung, William Morrow & Company, 1980

The World of Dragonflies and Damselflies, Ross E. Hutchins (entomologist), Dodd, Mead & Company, 1969

CHAPTERS IN BOOKS

Insects of the World, Anthony Wootton, Facts on File Publications, 1984

Introducing Insects, "Dragonflies," James G. Needham (professor of entomology, wrote field book on dragonflies), The Jaques Cattell Press, 1940, pp. 26–31

An Introduction to the Aquatic Insects of North America, "Odonata" entry written by Minter J. Westfall, Jr. (professor emeritus, University of Florida, expert on dragonflies and damselflies), Kendall/Hunt Publishing Company, 1984, pp. 126–176

Life on a Little Known Planet, "Water Lizards and Aerial Dragons," Howard Ensign Evans (entomologist), E.P. Dutton & Co., 1966, pp. 62–81

The Practical Entomologist, Rick Imes, Simon & Schuster, 1992, pp. 68–73

FIELD GUIDES

American Insects, a Handbook of the Insects of America North of Mexico, Ross H. Arnett, Jr. (research taxonomist), 1985, pp. 92–103

A Guide to Observing Insect Lives, Stokes Nature Guides, Donald W. Stokes, Little, Brown and Co., 1983, pp. 112–125

Insects of the Great Lakes Region, Gary A. Dunn (entomologist–MSU), University of Michigan, 1996, pp. 68–75

Simon & Schuster's Guide to Insects, Ross H. Arnett, Jr. and Richard L. Jacques, Jr., Simon & Schuster, 1981

WEB

"All About Dragonflies," Science Bytes, University of Tennessee

"Damsels and Dragons—the Insect Order Odonata," Ron Lyons, naturalist

"Dragonfly," Judi Manning, Owashtanong Islands Audubon Society, 1997

"Odonata," John W.H. Trueman and Richard J. Rowe (biology and zoology professors in Australia)

"The Odonata of North America," Dragonfly Society of the Americas

"Odonata of Japan," T. Aoki

ENCYCLOPEDIAS

The Audubon Society Encyclopedia of Animal Life, 1982

Compton's Encyclopedia online

Encyclopedia Americana, 1995, entry written by Minter Westfall, Jr.

Encyclopedia of Animals, 1972, edited by Dr. Maurice Burton

Grzimek's Animal Life Encyclopedia, Vol. 2, Insects, 1974, pp. 80–88

The Marshall Cavendish International Wildlife Encyclopedia, 1988

"Mayflies and Dragonflies," *Encyclopedia of Insects*, 1986

"On Wings of Gauze," *The Illustrated Encyclopedia of Wildlife*, 1991, pp. 2349–2362

MAGAZINE ARTICLES

"Darners That Dazzle," *World & I*, June 1996, Vol. 11, pp. 162+

"Dragonflies Are an Odd Combination of Beautiful Things," *Smithsonian*, July 1996, pp. 70+

"Dragonfly Invasion," *Science Activities*, Winter 1990, pp. 8+

"Dragons of the Air," *Nature Canada*, Summer 1996

"Those Colorful Needles with Shimmering Wings," *Conservationist*, August 1996, pp. 14+

"Zoom Along, Dragonfly!" *Cricket*, July 1994, pp. 35+

MUSEUMS

Smithsonian Institution
Washington, DC

INDEX